Coloring Techniques
for Paper Crafts™

Keri Lee Sereika

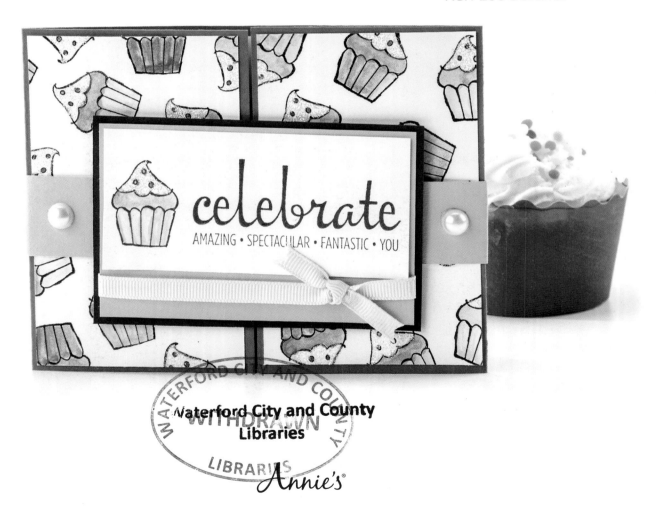

celebrate

AMAZING • SPECTACULAR • FANTASTIC • YOU

Annie's

Techniques

5 Alcohol Ink Markers

9 Watercolor

14 Colored Pencils

18 Chalks & Pastels

18 Chalk Coloring
22 Poppin' Pastels
24 Pullin' Pastels

26 Using Gelatos With Stencils, Sponges & Spritzes

26 Stenciling With Gelatos
29 Gelatos Sponging & Color Mixing
32 Gelatos VersaMark Resist

33 Glitter

33 Stamped Glitter Background
34 Glitter Window
38 Adhesive Glittered Embellishments
42 Adhesive Glitter Background

43 Heat Embossing

44 Embossing Basics
45 Embossing Basics With a Twist
48 Emboss Resist
50 Embossing Faux Metal

Cards

8   Thanks Very Much

12   Watercolor Flower

17   So Thankful

21   Birthday Celebration

23   Sorry You're Sick!

25   Celebrate

28   Make Today Ridiculously Amazing

30   Butterfly Lace

36   Good Luck

40   Never Forgotten

47   You're the Best

49   You Make My Heart Flutter

52   Happy Birthday to You!

4 Welcome   •   **4** Author Bio   •   **54** Paper-Crafting Basics   •   **56** Buyer's Guide

Welcome

"The purest and most thoughtful minds are those which love color the most."
—**John Ruskin**, *The Stones of Venice*

Color. Color is all around us. We take note of it in nature, fashion, art, home decor, etc. The subtle hues of color are often what excite us or deter us. One may love the color aqua, yet teal holds no inspiration. So many times one is inspired and has a need to express that inspiration. For some the art of applying color is exactly what is needed. Following on the heels of my first book, *Coloring Techniques for Card Making™*, my aim for this book is to inspire you and educate you on a variety of coloring techniques, all the while challenging you to "think outside the box" of your normal routine or your known coloring techniques. From the basics in watercolor, colored pencil and alcohol ink markers to the application of chalks, embossing powders, glitter and more, my sincerest hope is that you find the pages ahead of you filled with helpful information, thoughtful tips and pleasant, even surprising, inspiration!

Author Bio

Keri Lee, currently living in South Carolina, is a stay-at-home mother of four and wife to an airline pilot who also serves in the U.S. Air Force Reserve. She has authored crafting articles for a variety of magazines and online media, and she has had her designs featured in numerous publications. When she's not busy playing with her kids, you'll find Keri Lee in her studio creating projects or researching and writing articles on crafting. Keri Lee has published two additional books, *Exquisite Embellishments for Paper Crafts* and *Coloring Techniques for Card Making*. She is also the instructor for several Annie's Online Classes in beading, jewelry making and coloring techniques, all of which can be found at AnniesOnlineClasses.com.

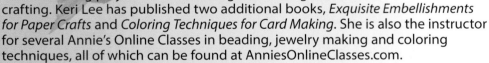

Alcohol Ink Markers

"Color is a means of exerting direct influence on the soul. Color is the keyboard, the eyes are the hammers, the soul is the piano with many strings. The artist is the hand which plays, touching one key or another purposively to cause vibrations in the soul."

—Wassily Kandinsky

Still one of the hottest techniques for coloring stamped images, alcohol ink markers are now readily available from many different manufacturers. Each manufacturer has a slightly different marker body and/or brush or tips on their markers, but the basic steps to applying color to a stamped image remain the same.

Along with alcohol ink markers you will need two additional items to learn how to color stamped images—a non-solvent-based ink pad and smooth-surface cardstock. A high quality, dye-based detail ink will allow you to stamp a crisp, clean impression that will dry quickly without the use of a heat tool to fully set it. A good smooth-surface cardstock with tightly woven fibers is key to blending colors well. Because the ink formula in alcohol ink markers can affect the ink of the stamped image, causing it to bleed, run or smudge while being colored, take time to test the ink and cardstock combinations you plan on using prior to beginning your project.

You Will Need:
- Stampin' Up! white cardstock
- Scrap paper
- Stampin' Up! stamp sets: By the Tide, Fabulous Four
- Imagine Crafts/Tsukineko Memento ink pads: rich cocoa, summer sky
- Copic® markers: R11, R14, R27
- Copic® Colorless Blender
- Craft sponge

As you can see in the materials photo, I have already created my palette and chosen the light, medium and dark shades of red and pink that work best for my image. ***Note:*** *If you are just beginning, sometimes it is best to start with an image that has a sense of "shading" already there and use it as a guide when applying your color.*

Alcohol Ink Markers

1. Begin by stamping your image onto smooth cardstock. Allow ink to dry completely. Begin to apply color starting with the lightest color (Photo 1).

2. Apply color using small circular motions until the paper is fully saturated through to the back side. Fully saturating the paper will help when you begin to blend in the deeper, darker colors (Photo 2).

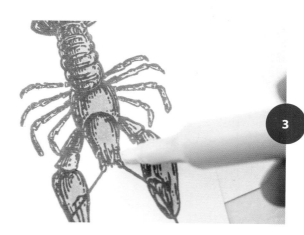

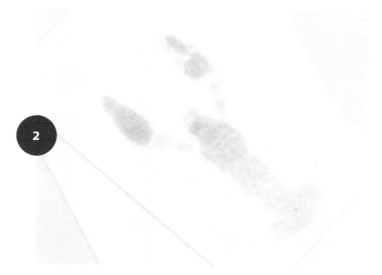

4. Prior to applying the additional layers of color, I prefer to loosen all of the caps on the markers of the color set I will be working with. This allows me to easily pick up and blend with the lighter colors as soon as I am done adding in my deeper, darker layers (Photo 4).

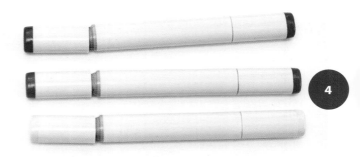

5. Apply the medium-tone color to the shaded portions of the image, overlapping just a bit into the more open areas of the image (Photo 5).

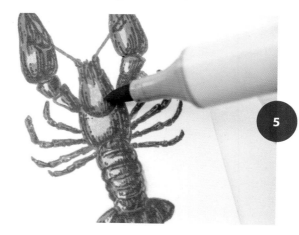

3. Having a Colorless Blender on hand is a helpful tool for fixing where you might color outside the lines. Simply place the edge of the Colorless Blender onto the stamped panel and "push the color" back toward the stamped image outer lines. Think of it this way, the Colorless "Blender" doesn't blend the colors; it really acts more like an eraser or a "pusher of color" (Photo 3).

6. Using the lightest color that had been used as the base color, go in and soften the lines by blending over the edges of the medium tone, again using that small circular motion to blend (Photo 6).

7. Finally, apply the darkest color to the deepest shaded areas and blend with first the medium-tone marker and then finally the lightest-tone marker. Apply more or less color as your preferences dictate (Photo 7).

8. Once you have finished coloring your image, add interest and depth by simply stamping on top of the image with a fine texture image and a very pale ink (Photo 8).

9. As a way of giving your finished image that "final boost," try adding a dark edge by applying color using a sponge (Photo 9). Begin by placing the sponge onto the scrap paper beneath your image, and then use a small pouncing motion as you work your way toward the edge of the stamped panel. Repeat by applying ink to the sponge and working from the scrap paper to the image's edge until the entire border is fully sponged (Photo 10).

Thanks Very Much

1. Form a 9½ x 4-inch card from light brown cardstock.

2. Cut a 9¼ x 3¾-inch piece from light brown patterned paper. Cut a 9¼ x 1¼-inch piece from navy cardstock; tear off bottom edge. Adhere to patterned paper panel. Cut a 9¼ x ½-inch piece from light blue patterned paper; adhere to navy strip. Wrap panel with baker's twine; tie in a double bow. Adhere panel to card front.

3. Stamp lobster image onto white cardstock using brown ink; color with markers. Stamp script image over lobster image using blue ink. Sponge edges of panel brown. Adhere panel to brown cardstock; trim a small border. Attach to card front using foam squares.

4. Die-cut a 2⅞-inch Labels One shape from white cardstock. Stamp sentiment using brown ink. Cut die-cut shape horizontally just below sentiment. Adhere sentiment to card front.

5. Thread buttons with linen thread; tie in a knot on back, trim ends. Attach buttons to card front using adhesive dots. ✘

Designer's Tip:

Stamping a second image over top of the main image creates the look of both depth and texture. Further enhance the image by distressing and sponging the edges of the panel prior to layering on a mat.

Materials

- Stampin' Up! cardstock: soft suede, night of navy, chocolate chip, whisper white
- Die Cuts With A View 12 x 12 paper pads: Midnight Berry, Coral and Navy
- Stampin' Up! stamp sets: By the Tide, Fabulous Four
- Imagine Crafts/Tsukineko Memento ink pads: rich cocoa, summer sky
- Copic® markers: R11, R14, R27
- Copic® Colorless Blender
- The Twinery cappuccino baker's twine
- 2 red buttons
- Linen thread
- Spellbinders™ Labels One die templates (#S4-161)
- Die-cutting machine
- Craft sponge
- Adhesive foam squares
- Adhesive dots
- Paper adhesive

Watercolor

"Color does not add a pleasant quality to design—it reinforces it."
—Pierre Bonnard

One of the first coloring mediums we are exposed to as children is watercolor. Why do you think that is? It is because watercolors are a forgiving medium that often bring just the right amount of color to any piece they are applied to. There are a few things you should know about the art of watercoloring a stamped image. In this book we will be using watercolor pencils in our step-by-step photos. However, later in the book you will see two additional processes used to watercolor with chalk and ink. The technique of using varying amounts of water to "float" color onto an image is very similar, no matter which medium of color you choose. However, take note of the different outcomes. You will find that each has its own distinctive finished look.

The tools used for watercoloring stamped images are very simple and basic. You will need a color medium (we have already mentioned watercolor pencils, ink and chalks). There are also watercolor paints, watercolor crayons, watercolor sheets and more. In addition to the color medium, you will need water and a brush, paper or cardstock, waterproof ink, a stamp to create the image and a palette of sorts. There are many varieties of each of these items listed, but I would like to discuss the items I find most important to understand.

Let's start with the water and brush. I prefer to use a watercolor brush and a small jar of water when watercoloring. However, there are also brush pens that others I know love and use almost exclusively. A brush pen is simply a pen with an empty barrel and a brush on the end. The barrel can be filled with water and gently squeezed to control the flow of water being used in the application.

The type of paper or cardstock used is very important. You will need a thick cardstock or watercolor paper. Watercolor paper is known by its rough or "toothy" texture and will help give your project an authentic watercolor look. It is this texture that also allows the paper to capture pigment and water without causing the paper to pucker or curl.

Two more items that I feel are important to mention are the waterproof ink and the use of a palette. The importance of choosing a waterproof ink that will not run or feather when water is applied over top of it is *crucial* to success in watercoloring a stamped image. There are many waterproof inks available on the market. Some are solvent based; some are pigment based.

And finally, the palette. You will notice I often use a palette in my creative process, not just with watercoloring. I like to think of it as a "test spot" for mixing colors, testing out color combinations, and helping to moderate how much color is used as well as to what depth that color is applied. A palette can be piece of paper to scribble excess color onto or a nonporous item to place ink or paint on, such as a plate or old CD.

Watercolor

You Will Need:
- Watercolor paper
- Stampin' Up! Backyard Basics stamp set
- Imagine Crafts/Tsukineko StazOn jet black ink pad
- Fantasia premium watercolor pencils
- Stampin' Up! Backyard Basics die set (#129380)
- Die-cutting machine
- Royal & Langnickel watercolor brush
- Paper towels

1. Stamp image onto watercolor paper and die-cut. If you are using an image without a specific die, you can "fussy cut" around the image. I prefer to cut my image out first and then color so that I don't accidentally ruin an image I have spent time watercoloring. Also, create a palette using the colors you plan to mix and use (Photo 1).

2. With a moistened brush, touch the tip of the brush into the scribbled color on the palette to load the first color onto your brush (Photo 2).

3. Remove excess color and moisture from the brush tip by gently touching it to a piece of paper towel or napkin (Photo 3).

4. Using gentle strokes, apply first layer of color to flower petals and buds (Photo 4).

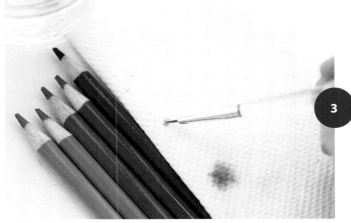

5. Using varying amounts of water, paint some areas of the image lighter than others for that true watercolor effect (Photo 5).

6. After thoroughly rinsing the brush, apply color to the stems of the flowers in the same fashion (Photo 6).

7. Begin mixing colors on the palette to apply the second layer of color (Photo 7).

8. Apply the second layer of color to the flower and buds, working on deepening the darkest areas and accentuating the lightest areas, bringing the image to life. If a third or fourth layer of color is desired or needed, simply allow the paper surface to dry between applications to avoid creating a softened or soggy surface (Photo 8).

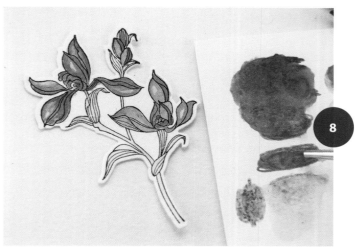

9. Apply additional color to the stems and leaves to finish your watercolor image (Photo 9).

Watercolor Flower

1. Form a 4¼ x 5½-inch card from light brown cardstock.

2. Cut a 3¾ x 5-inch piece from yellow cardstock, stamp flower image three times across top third of panel using watermark ink. Sew a zigzag stitch across top of panel.

3. Cut a 3¾ x 2-inch piece from yellow patterned paper; adhere to stamped panel. Cut a 3¾ x ¾-inch piece from rust patterned paper; adhere to panel. Wrap ribbon around panel. Tie in a knot; trim ends.

4. Adhere panel to brown cardstock; trim a small border. Adhere to card front.

5. Stamp flower image onto watercolor paper using black ink. Die-cut around image using corresponding die shape. Color image using watercolors and brush. Attach to card front using foam squares.

6. Attach self-adhesive pearls as shown. ✘

Designer's Tip:

The design of this card is easily reproduced using any floral image of your choice. The same cutout effect can be done by simply stamping the image and using sharp paper snips to "fussy cut" around the image.

Materials

- Stampin' Up! cardstock: baked brown sugar, chocolate chip, so saffron
- Die Cuts With A View Brooklyn 12 x 12 paper pad
- Watercolor paper
- Stampin' Up! Backyard Basics stamp set
- Imagine Crafts/ Tsukineko ink pads: VersaMark (watermark), StazOn (jet black)
- Fantasia premium watercolor pencils
- 12 inches ¼-inch-wide brown grosgrain ribbon
- Queen & Co. cream self-adhesive pearls
- Stampin' Up! Backyard Basics die set (#129380)
- Die-cutting machine
- Royal & Langnickel watercolor brush
- Sewing machine with white thread
- Paper towels
- Adhesive foam squares
- Paper adhesive

Colored Pencils

"Sunset is still my favorite color, and rainbow is second."

—**Mattie Stepanek**

The most controlled and perhaps the most forgiving technique used to color in line art images is, in my humble opinion, the colored pencil technique. Understanding the difference in pencil qualities, as well as how that affects the outcome of the finished piece, may help you decide which type of colored pencil is best suited for this technique.

The "lead" or core of a colored pencil is comprised of a mixture of pigment (color), wax and fillers. The ratio of pigment to wax and fillers depends heavily on the quality of the pencil you have. Typically, artist-quality colored pencils have more pigment, and less wax and fillers than cheaper colored pencils. The "leads" also tend to be softer and easier to blend. The technique demonstrated uses artist-quality colored pencils; however, feel free to use whatever colored pencils you have on hand. If you only have "craft-quality" colored pencils, the biggest difference you will notice is that the leads tend to be harder and may not leave as much pigment on the surface of the cardstock as a higher-quality pencil. Therefore, you may need additional layers of color to create the depth you are hoping to achieve.

The wax-based "leads" of colored pencils can be broken down using a blending agent. The most commonly used is artist-grade odorless mineral spirits (OMS). The color can then be blended or moved along the surface of the paper using a tool called an artist blending stump. A stump is a tool used for application and blending, and it is comprised of compressed paper pulp. The pulp is then pressed into a dense tube and sharpened on both ends. A stump can be cleaned off and resharpened with the use of a sanding strip or sanding block. When looking for blending stumps, don't be fooled into purchasing tortillions. Tortillions are also used for blending, but they are tightly wrapped, hollow, paper-blending instruments. And while they are created for blending, they will not soak up the blending agent the way a blending stump will; therefore, they will not produce the same outcome.

The use of smooth-surface cardstock is also important for ease of blending. The tightly woven fibers allow the pigment to be broken down and blended across the surface, whereas a lesser-quality, rougher-surface cardstock can be difficult to work with because the pigment tends to stay where you put it and will not blend out as nicely.

Note: *If you are wary of working with odorless mineral spirits, are pregnant or have an allergy to it, pure baby oil can be used instead for this technique. It must be used sparingly so as to not stain the image you are working on, so a bit of experimentation should be done to find out just how much oil is needed to break down the wax and fillers in the colored pencil "leads."*

You Will Need:

- Stampin' Up! whisper white cardstock
- Stampin' Up! Sweet Stuff stamp set
- Imagine Crafts/Tsukineko Memento ink pads: tuxedo black, summer sky
- Prismacolor colored pencils: mulberry, lime peel, Spanish orange
- Gamblin Gamsol odorless mineral spirits (OMS)
- Blending stumps
- Sanding stick

1. Prior to beginning to color, it's a good idea to get your stumps clean of residual color from previous projects. To do this, simply swipe the tip of the stump at an angle against the sanding stick (Photo 1). Continue to gently roll the stump a bit with each swipe so as to both remove the remaining color as well as sharpen the tip of the stump (Photo 2).

2. Apply a heavy line of color to the center of the flower and the leaves of the flower. A little bit of color goes a long way, and we will be adding additional color in following steps (Photo 3).

3. Roll or dip the tip of your blending stump in the OMS until it is fully saturated but not dripping. Here you can see I have a bottle with a dauber top. If you don't have access to a bottle like this, you can moisten a small square of a sponge and then just press the tip of the blending stump into the sponge (Photo 4).

4. Using small circular motions, begin to spread and blend the color in toward the center of the image (Photo 5).

5. Clean the blending stump or use a different end to blend the color applied to the leaves. Again, a small circular motion is best, but if the image you are working with has areas that are too small to go in circles, you can simply make small repetitive strokes to be sure all color is blended well (Photo 6).

6. Apply a heavy line of color to the flower petals. The reason we didn't apply the petal color along with the other colors was to assist in avoiding smearing the deeper fuchsia color into the pale yellow. Planning ahead and applying and blending lighter colors first will help to avoid unwanted smudging and smearing when working with images. Repeat the application of OMS and use the same circular motion to blend the petal color (Photo 7).

7. Once you have blended your first application of color, create a palette by scribbling the colors you are working with onto a piece of scrap paper. To deepen the color of the petals and leaves, simply rub the blending stump onto the color on the palette and apply the color to any area of the image where you wish to deepen the color (Photo 8).

8. To help ground an image like the one we are working with, take the blending stump and load it with the green color used for the leaves. Apply the color to the bottom of the image panel to create a softened "grass" look (Photo 9).

9. As a finishing touch, use a sponge and a pale blue ink to sponge the top three edges of the stamped panel (Photo 10).

So Thankful

1. Form a 4¼ x 4¼-inch card from green cardstock.

2. Cut a 4 x 4-inch piece from pink patterned paper. Cut a 4 x 1⅛-inch piece from striped patterned paper; adhere to pink panel. Wrap panel with a 5-inch length of ribbon as shown; adhering ends to back. Adhere panel to card front.

3. Working with remaining 4-inch length of ribbon, bring both ends to center overlapping slightly to create a loop. Pinch loop in center and tie with baker's twine to create a bow. Attach to card front using adhesive dot. Attach button to center of bow using adhesive dot.

4. Die-cut a 2⅜-inch Classic Scalloped Circles SM shape from navy cardstock. Die-cut a 2⅛-inch Standard Circles LG shape from light blue patterned paper. Layer and adhere circles to card front.

5. Cut a 1¼ x 2-inch piece from white cardstock. Stamp flower image onto cardstock piece; color using colored pencils and blend with OMS and blending stumps. Adhere to green cardstock; trim a small border. Adhere to card front.

6. Stamp sentiment onto white cardstock; color in the same manner as before. Cut out; attach to card front using foam squares. ✗

Materials

- Stampin' Up! cardstock: night of navy, old olive, whisper white
- Hampton Art KI Memories Playlist 6 x 6 paper pad
- Stampin' Up! stamp sets: Sweet Stuff, Amazing Birthday
- Imagine Crafts/ Tsukineko Memento ink pads: tuxedo black, summer sky
- Prismacolor colored pencils: mulberry, lime peel, Spanish orange
- 9 inches ⅝-inch-wide light pink grosgrain ribbon
- Buttons Galore cream pearl button
- Pink/white baker's twine
- Spellbinders™ die templates: Classic Scalloped Circles SM (#S4-125), Standard Circles SM (#S4-116)
- Die-cutting machine
- Gamblin Gamsol odorless mineral spirits (OMS)
- Sanding stick
- Blending stumps
- Cosmetic sponge
- Adhesive foam squares
- Paper adhesive

Chalks & Pastels

"Mere color, unspoiled by meaning, and unallied with definite form, can speak to the soul in a thousand different ways."

—Oscar Wilde

Chalk is a medium that is very versatile and can be applied in a large variety of ways. We could probably fill a book with ways to use chalks and other pigment powders. However, I thought it might be best to pick just a few popular ways to use chalks and quickly talk about additional applications.

In the upcoming step-by-step tutorials you will see that I am using two different types of chalks. One is a set of artist dry pastels and the others are pearlescent chalks that come in many different colors and varying shades. Each type of chalk has its own abilities and limitations, but overall the products used can be interchanged. If you have chalks at home, feel free to try the techniques you see here and see how your products work for each application. Some people are concerned about the chalk applied to their projects coming off onto other things such as hands and clothing. If you are concerned, a spray sealant can be applied in multiple light coats. You will find professional sealants in the art aisle, but you can also use an inexpensive aerosol hairspray and it will seal it enough to keep the chalk on the art, not on the hands!

Chalk Coloring

A great way to use the skills you learned in the Watercolor section of this book and add a touch of softness to your projects would be to watercolor using chalks as your color medium.

You Will Need:
- Stampin' Up! whisper white cardstock
- Stampin' Up! Sweet Stuff stamp set
- Imagine Crafts/Tsukineko StazOn jet black ink pad
- Sparkle N Sprinkle starfire glitter
- Reeves soft pastels
- Water brush
- Adhesive pen

1. Using a waterproof ink, stamp image randomly all over the panel, turning the image or the paper so that the images are sideways and upside down (Photo 1).

2. Using a water brush or a watercolor brush and container of water, lightly wet the brush and touch the very tip of the brush to the color of choice. Touch the tip of the brush to a piece of scrap paper before beginning to watercolor the images. This will allow you to see the color you plan to use as well as have better control of how much water and color will be transferred to the image you are going to color (Photo 2).

3. Using the same technique as when watercoloring with watercolor pencils, apply the color in layers adding color as needed to reach desired depth of color (Photo 3).

4. One fabulous aspect to chalks is that they are easily blended on a palette to create custom colors. Simply work the colors together with a bit of water to get the exact shade needed for the project. Here I have added a bit of bright green to the yellow that I was working with, and I have added a touch of black to the bright blue to mute it (Photo 4).

5. Use the custom colors to apply color to the rest of the bottoms of the cupcakes on the panel, cleaning the brush between colors (Photo 5).

6. Apply just a tiny dot of color to each sprinkle on the top of the cupcakes (Photo 6).

7. Use a lighter shade to color the middle section of the cupcake image. Now you could stop and the images would be cute, but we have a few more steps to really kick them up a notch (Photo 7).

8. Once the images have fully dried, use a glue pen to apply glue to the remaining white area of the image (Photo 8).

9. Working on just a few images at a time, apply glue and then shake on glitter, apply glue, shake on glitter until you have covered the entire panel (Photo 9).

10. Remove the excess glitter to reveal your chalk colored images highlighted with glitter (Photo 10).

Birthday Celebration

1. Cut an 11 x 4¼-inch piece from pink cardstock. With long side horizontal, score a vertical line 2¾ inches from each end; fold ends in to center to create a 5½ x 4¼-inch gatefold card.

2. Cut an 8½ x 5½-inch piece from white cardstock. Stamp randomly with cupcake image using black ink. Color images with pastels. Embellish using glitter and adhesive pen; let dry.

3. Cut two 2½ x 4-inch pieces from stamped panel; adhere one piece to each side panel of card front.

4. For card band, cut a 1 x 11-inch piece from aqua cardstock. Wrap piece around back of card bringing ends to front and creasing edges at sides.

5. Cut a 3⅝ x 1¾-inch piece from white cardstock. Stamp cupcake and sentiment onto panel using black ink. Color cupcake with markers; embellish using adhesive pen and glitter.

6. Adhere cupcake panel to aqua cardstock; trim a small border. Wrap bottom edge of panel with ribbon; tie in a knot and V-notch ends. Adhere to navy cardstock; trim a small border.

7. Attach assembled panel to card band using foam squares.

8. Attach pearls to band as shown. Slide band onto card. ✘

Materials

- Stampin' Up! cardstock: strawberry slush, coastal cabana, night of navy, whisper white
- Stampin' Up! stamp sets: Sweet Stuff, Fabulous Four
- Imagine Crafts/ Tsukineko StazOn jet black ink pad
- Sparkle N Sprinkle starfire glitter
- Reeves soft pastels
- 12 inches ¼-inch-wide light pink grosgrain ribbon
- Want2Scrap pale pink self-adhesive pearls
- Water brush
- Scoring board
- Adhesive pen
- Adhesive foam squares
- Paper adhesive

Poppin' Pastels

While the steps are few, the results are so very rewarding. Poppin' Pastels is a great technique to use to create a quick background panel for multiple cards at once, or to color a main image quickly using a variety of colors.

You Will Need:

- Stampin' Up! Sahara sand cardstock
- Stampin' Up! Petite Petals stamp set
- Imagine Crafts/ Tsukineko VersaMark watermark ink pad
- Pebbles Inc. Kan'dee pearlescent jewel tone chalk set
- Chalk applicator

1. Use VersaMark watermark ink to stamp images randomly over the entire panel, turning the image or the cardstock so that the images are not all facing the same direction (Photo 1).

2. Using a small pouncing motion, apply chalk to the surface of the image. Apply color only to the image, not fully covering the surface of the cardstock (Photo 2).

3. Once you have applied color to each image, gently blow away the excess chalk powder prior to moving on to the next step. This is very important to help reduce smudging (Photo 3).

4. Use a paper towel and a broad, light sweeping motion to gently wipe away any remaining chalk dust (Photo 4).

The finished piece can now be used as is, or you could fill it in with smaller images and apply a second, third, or more colors. The uses are limitless (Photo 5).

Note: Keeping a white art eraser on hand is very useful for easily removing stray bits of color that are sometimes left behind.

Sorry You're Sick!

1. Form a 4¼ x 5½-inch card from brown cardstock.

2. Cut a 3⅞ x 5⅛-inch piece from light brown cardstock. Using photo as a guide, stamp flower images onto light brown panel using watermark ink. Apply chalk to images. Adhere panel to pink cardstock; trim a small border. Adhere to card front.

3. Cut a 3⅞ x 2-inch piece from light orange cardstock. Stamp flower images onto piece using orange ink as shown; adhere to card front.

4. Cut a 3⅞ x 1-inch piece from white cardstock. Stamp sentiment onto white panel using brown ink. Adhere to pink cardstock; trim a small border along top and bottom edges.

5. Wrap baker's twine several times around left end of sentiment panel; secure ends to back. Attach panel to card front using foam squares.

6. Attach butterfly to card front using foam squares. ✘

Materials
- Stampin' Up! cardstock: soft suede, Sahara sand, crisp cantaloupe, strawberry slush, whisper white
- Stampin' Up! stamp sets: Petite Petals, Fabulous Four
- Ink pads: Imagine Crafts/Tsukineko Memento (rich cocoa), VersaMark (watermark); Stampin' Up! (crisp cantaloupe)
- Pebbles Inc. pearlescent jewel tone chalk set
- The Twinery mandarin baker's twine
- Jillibean Soup Sunshine corrugated shapes
- Chalk applicator
- Adhesive foam squares
- Paper adhesive

Pullin' Pastels

A very similar technique to Poppin' Pastels, Pullin' Pastels works in the opposite direction. Apply chalk first, then "pull" it off the cardstock using stamps inked with VersaMark watermark ink.

You Will Need:

- Stampin' Up! basic black cardstock
- Stampin' Up! By The Tide stamp set
- Imagine Crafts/ Tsukineko VersaFine watermark ink pad
- Pebbles Inc. Kan'dee Shimmers pearlescent chalk set
- Cosmetic sponge wedge

1. Using a cosmetic sponge wedge, evenly apply chalk to the surface of the entire cardstock panel (Photo 1).

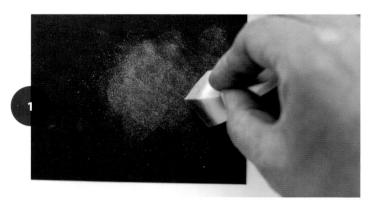

2. Using VersaMark watermark ink, stamp the fine script image onto the panel, cleaning the stamp and reinking between each impression (Photo 2).

3. Use the largest image to stamp the collage of images, taking care to clean the stamp and reink between each impression (Photo 3).

4. Use the next-largest image planned for the collage, again making sure to clean and reink the stamp between impressions (Photo 4).

5. Finish the panel using the final and smallest image. Seal if desired (Photo 5).

Materials

- Stampin' Up! cardstock: real red, basic black, whisper white
- Die Cuts With A View Limoncello 12 x 12 paper pad
- Stampin' Up! stamp sets: By The Tide, Fabulous Four
- Imagine Crafts/Tsukineko ink pads: Memento (tuxedo black), VersaMark (watermark)
- Pebbles Inc. Shimmers pearlescent chalk set
- 18 inches ⅝-inch-wide double-stitched red grosgrain ribbon
- Queen & Co. red self-adhesive rhinestones
- Cosmetic sponge
- Paper piercer
- Foam piercing mat
- Adhesive foam squares
- Paper adhesive

Celebrate

1. Form a 5¼ x 5¼-inch card from red cardstock.

2. Cut a 5 x 5-inch piece from black cardstock; adhere to card front.

3. Cut a 4¾ x 4¾-inch piece from gray and white patterned paper.

4. Cut a 2¾ x 4¾-inch piece from black cardstock; sponge with shimmery gray chalk. Starting with the finest images followed by heavier images and cleaning the stamp between each impression, pull images from the panel using the Pullin' Pastels technique from Chalks & Pastels tutorial (see page 24).

5. Tear off bottom edge of stamped panel; adhere to patterned paper panel. Wrap panel with ribbon; tie in a bow. Adhere to card front.

6. Cut a 2¾ x 1¾-inch piece from white cardstock. Stamp sentiment onto cardstock piece using black ink.

7. Pierce holes along bottom edge of cardstock panel using piercing tool. Attach to red cardstock with foam squares; trim a small border. Attach to card front using foam squares.

8. Embellish card with rhinestones as shown. ✘

Using Gelatos With Stencils, Sponges & Spritzes

"The lyf so short, the craft so long to lerne."
—Geoffrey Chaucer

In this chapter, I wanted to teach a few techniques that have many different applications: stenciling, sponging and spritzing. All of these words are hot in the paper-crafting industry, and many manufacturers have their own versions of products that are created just for these purposes. In this chapter I thought it would be great to showcase a relatively new product called Gelatos. Water-soluble pigment in a lip-balm–like tube, Gelatos have many different applications. I chose to show a few and point out other areas where they come in handy too!

Stenciling With Gelatos

In this technique you will learn how to use the Gelatos in a classic stencil application of pouncing with a round flat-ended brush. However, an alternative would be to spritz the color onto the surface. That could be done using premade spritz sprays, or you could make your own using shavings of Gelatos, adding water in a spray bottle, and shaking well until all the color is dissolved. For this application I found

I liked the outcome when using the stencil, a stencil brush, a palette and the Gelatos.

You Will Need:
- Stampin' Up! whisper white cardstock
- Faber-Castell Earl Grey Gelato
- Hampton Art Stamp and Stencil Butterflies stencil
- Faber-Castell stipple brush
- Spray bottle

1. Begin by scribbling a heavy layer of Gelatos onto a nonporous surface. Here I am using a piece of acetate from the back of a stamp set. Spray the surface lightly with water (Photo 1).

2. Load the brush with color by swirling through and pouncing onto the moistened color. If additional color or water is necessary, simply add more to be sure the entire edge of the brush is filled with color. Place the stencil over the cardstock panel to be stenciled and press lightly all over the surface to be sure it is well adhered (Photo 2).

3. Holding the brush perpendicular to the paper below, pounce straight down starting at the center of the stencil and working your way out toward the edges (Photo 3).

4. Continue reloading the brush with color as necessary as you continue applying the color in a pouncing motion. Be sure to go out past the edges of the panel beneath the stencil in order to have a fully stenciled piece (Photo 4).

5. Slowly peel the stencil away from the now stenciled piece. Check the edges to be sure you have full coverage. If you find you have uneven application of color or missed some areas, carefully lay the stencil back in place and repeat the color application (Photo 5).

6. Allow the piece to fully dry before using it so as to allow the color to fully set and not smudge or run (Photo 6).

Make Today Ridiculously Amazing

1. Form a 5½ x 4¼-inch card from gray cardstock.

2. Cut a 5¼ x 4-inch piece from black cardstock; adhere to card front.

3. Cut a 5 x 3¾-inch piece from gray and white patterned paper.

4. Cut a 1¾ x 3¾-inch piece from white cardstock. Using Gelatos and stipple brush, stencil pattern onto panel; adhere to patterned paper panel. Wrap ribbon around panel as shown; tie in a bow and V-notch ends. Adhere to card front.

5. For sentiment panel, cut a 2 x 3-inch piece from white cardstock. Ink the word "AMAZING" using red marker. Ink remainder of image using black ink pad. "Huff" onto inked stamp to reactivate inks; stamp onto panel. Adhere to red cardstock; trim a small border. Adhere to card front. ✘

Materials

- Cardstock: Bazzill Basics (gray); Stampin' Up! (basic black, real red, whisper white)
- Die Cuts With A View Limoncello 12 x 12 paper pad
- Stampin' Up! Amazing Birthday stamp set
- Imagine Crafts/ Tsukineko Memento tuxedo black ink pad
- Faber-Castell Earl Grey Gelato
- Tombow crimson marker
- 18 inches Really Reasonable Ribbon ⅝-inch-wide red check ribbon
- Hampton Art Stamp and Stencil Butterflies stencil
- Spray bottle
- Faber-Castell stippling brush
- Paper adhesive

Gelatos Sponging & Color Mixing

A great feature of Gelatos is that they can be applied in so many different ways, and they can be mixed to create custom colors. The mixing can be done on the palette prior to application of the project or it can be done on the project itself by simply overlapping the colors when applied. Here I will show you how a very quick sponging of the first color and then applying a second color, overlapping at the edges, can create beautiful end results.

You Will Need:

- Stampin' Up! whisper white cardstock
- Hampton Art stamp Stamp & Stencil Butterflies stamp set
- Imagine Crafts/ Tsukineko StazOn jet black ink pad
- Faber-Castell Gelatos: snow cone, tropical raspberry
- Craft sheet
- Spray bottle
- Cosmetic sponges
- Paper towels

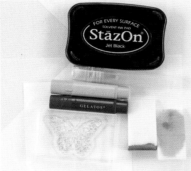

1. Stamp image using waterproof ink; allow to fully dry. Create a palette using a sheet of acetate. Hold the Gelato at an angle and roll the edge in one spot to create a small pile of shavings (Photo 1).

2. Spritz each pile with water. Load the sponges with color. Add more water to the piles of color as necessary (Photo 2).

3. Begin in the center of the image and sponge right down the center, top to bottom (Photo 3).

4. Working quickly to get the best blending ability, apply the second color to outer edges of the image. Use both pouncing motions and swirling motions to apply, and then blend the colors respectively (Photo 4).

5. Repeat the color applications until the image has the desired depth of color (Photo 5).

Butterfly Lace

1. Form a 4¼ x 5½-inch card from purple cardstock.

2. Cut a 3¾ x 2¾-inch piece from white cardstock. Stamp flourish images using watermark ink; allow a minute for ink to set.

3. Use cosmetic sponge and purple Gelato to apply color to stamped panel. Gently rub off Gelato with a paper towel to reveal the resist image. Adhere panel to black cardstock; trim a small border. Adhere to card front as shown.

4. Cut a 3¾ x ½-inch piece from white cardstock. Following steps 2 and 3, repeat resist technique using blue Gelato. Adhere cardstock piece to card front as shown.

5. Cut a 1¾ x 1¾-inch piece from white cardstock. Stamp butterfly image using black ink, allowing image to extend past edges. Adhere to black cardstock; trim a small border. Adhere to card front.

6. Stamp script print butterfly onto white cardstock. Using photo as a guide, apply color to butterfly image using Gelatos and cosmetic sponge; cut out. Attach butterfly to card front using foam squares.

7. Adhere lace to card front.

8. Cut a ½ x 4¾-inch piece from black cardstock; crimp using paper crimper. Adhere to card front; trim to fit. Attach rhinestones as shown.

9. Cut a 4 x 2¼-inch piece from blue cardstock; stamp sentiment using watermark ink. Sprinkle with embossing powder; heat-emboss. Slide panel underneath lace on card and adhere in place.

Materials
- Cardstock: Die Cuts With A View (pastels stack); Stampin' Up! (basic black, whisper white)
- Hampton Art stamp sets: Stamp & Stencil Butterflies, Occasions
- Imagine Crafts/ Tsukineko ink pads: VersaMark (watermark), StazOn (jet black)
- Clear embossing powder
- Faber-Castell Gelatos: snow cone, tropical raspberry
- 4¼ inches 1¼-inch-wide white lace
- Clear self-adhesive rhinestones
- Cosmetic sponge
- Paper towels
- Craft sheet
- Spray bottle
- Paper crimper
- Embossing heat tool
- Faber-Castell Dot Dabber tool
- Scrapbook Adhesives by 3L® adhesive foam squares
- Paper adhesive

Designer's Tip:
Instead of stamping a sentiment on blue cardstock, another option is to stamp a sentiment onto a die-cut panel and adhere it to the card. A great way to always have the right card ready is to make a stock of generic note cards and add the proper sentiment as needed.

happy birthday

Gelatos VersaMark Resist

You Will Need:

- Stampin' Up! whisper white cardstock
- Hampton Art stamp Stamp & Stencil Butterflies stamp set
- Imagine Crafts/ Tsukineko VersaMark watermark ink pad
- Faber-Castell tropical raspberry Gelato
- Cosmetic sponge
- Paper towels

Working with the palette created with the previous technique, I am going to teach a resist technique. While using a process very similar to the Emboss Resist technique on page 48, VersaMark Resist eliminates embossing, and the outcome is a very batik-like finished look. The images are light and soft.

1. Use VersaMark watermark ink to stamp images on the entire panel of cardstock (Photo 1).

2. Sponge color over top of the stamped images (Photo 2).

3. Use a paper towel to remove the excess color (Photo 3).

4. The effect is a piece that can be used as shown, or this can now be stamped onto with a darker color of ink to create a double-layered background paper (Photo 4). ✗

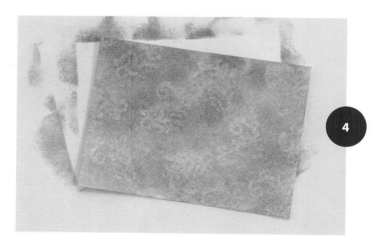

Note: *Try using a glossy cardstock and ink for this technique. The images will be much more pronounced and visible. While still using the same technique, you will note it has a very different end result by simply changing those two products.*

Glitter

"You can't use up creativity. The more you use, the more you have."
—Maya Angelou

Even the best design can sometimes lack that special something, that finishing touch. Often a hint of sparkle can be that perfect "Ta-da!" to the finished project. We tend to overlook the power a little bit of glitter can wield. While throwing a bit of glitter haphazardly can sometimes do the trick, in this chapter we will take a look at how to purposefully use glitter in a variety of ways from main image enhancement to creative backgrounds and more.

Stamped Glitter Background

Although this seems a simple two-step technique, it is one that often goes overlooked. I felt it simply had to be a part of the book!

You Will Need:

- Die Cuts With A View pastel green cardstock
- Impression Obsession Cover-a-Card Dots stamp
- Sparkle N Sprinkle green nugget glitter
- Imagine Crafts/Tsukineko glue pad

1. Use a glue stamp pad or a folded paper towel moistened with watered-down craft glue to "ink" the stamp. Stamp the top half of the cardstock panel and cover it immediately with glitter (Photo 1).

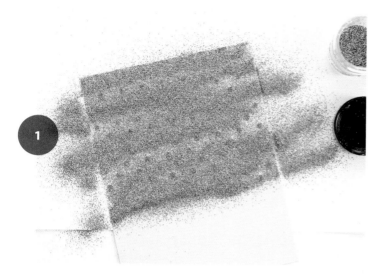

2. Remove the excess glitter and allow the panel to dry completely (Photo 2).

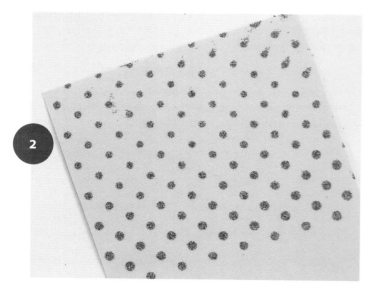

Glitter Window

Using basic paper-crafting supplies and a roll of clear household packing tape makes this a fun and simple technique for adding a bit of sparkle to any card! And while this showcases the use of a simple circle punch, don't limit yourself to just a circle; any punch smaller than the 2-inch width of the packing tape will work. Some have even used clear contact paper in place of the tape, and at that point the sky is the limit as to what shapes and sizes you can make your glitter window!

You Will Need:

- Stampin' Up! very vanilla cardstock
- Hampton Art Stamp and Stencil Occasions stamp set
- Clearsnap blue iris chalk ink pad
- Sparkle N Sprinkle starfire glitter
- EK Success 1⅜-inch circle punch
- Clear packing tape

1. Use a punch to create a hole in the panel (Photo 3).

2. Place the panel facedown onto a smooth surface. Here I am using a stamp block. Place a piece of packing tape over the hole in the panel and press all around the window to fully secure the tape (Photo 4).

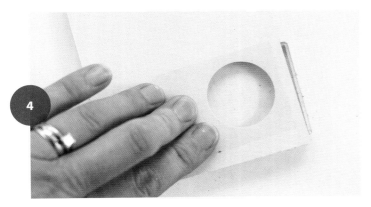

3. Turn the panel over and remove the stamp block if it is stuck to the tape. Cover the tape with a fine translucent glitter (Photo 5).

4. Remove the excess glitter to reveal the glitter window. Make sure the entire surface is well covered with glitter (Photo 6).

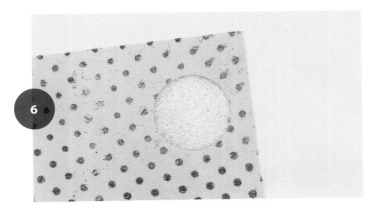

5. Turn the panel back over and place a small piece of adhesive above and below the glitter window. Line up the sentiment beneath the glitter window (Photo 7).

6. Press above and below the stamped image to adhere it behind the glitter window (Photo 8).

Good Luck

1. Form a 4¼ x 5½-inch card from purple cardstock.

2. Cut a 4 x 5¼-inch piece from light green cardstock, stamp top half of panel using glue pad and Dots Cover a Card stamp. ***Note:*** *Clean stamp immediately after use to prevent glue from drying on stamp surface.* Sprinkle green glitter on top of dots; tap to remove excess. Let dry.

3. Wrap ribbon around left side of panel; tie in a double bow. Using heat tool, carefully heat bow until ribbon begins to crumple slightly.

4. Referring to photo, punch circle from glittered panel. Cover opening with packing tape attaching tape to back of panel with sticky side facing front. Sprinkle exposed tape with starfire glitter creating a glitter window.

5. Cut a 2 x 2-inch piece from ivory cardstock; stamp sentiment using blue ink. Adhere to back side of glittered panel, centering sentiment within glitter window. Adhere panel to ivory cardstock; trim a small border. Adhere to card front.

6. Cut a 4 x 2-inch piece from light blue patterned paper; adhere to card front as shown.

7. Cut a 4 x 1-inch piece from pink patterned paper; adhere to card front.

8. Attach green buttons to card front as shown using adhesive dots. ✗

Designer's Tip:

You can create a one-time-use "glue pad" by folding up a paper towel into the size of a stamp pad and wetting it generously with slightly watered-down craft glue. Be sure to fully saturate the paper towel but not to the point of it being dripping wet, thereby allowing too much glue to transfer to the stamp.

Materials
- Cardstock: Die Cuts With A View (pastel green); Stampin' Up! (very vanilla, rich razzleberry)
- Hampton Art KI Memories Playlist 6 x 6 paper pad
- Stamp sets: Impression Obsession (Cover a Card Dots); Hampton Art (Stamp and Stencil Occasions)
- Clearsnap blue iris chalk ink pad
- Sparkle N Sprinkle glitter: green nugget, starfire
- 24 inches Morex ⅝-inch-wide ivory organza ribbon
- 10 Buttons Galore small spring green buttons
- Embossing heat tool
- EK Success 1⅜-inch circle punch
- Clear packing tape
- Imagine Crafts/ Tsukineko glue pad
- Adhesive dots
- Paper adhesive

Adhesive Glittered Embellishments

Creating handmade glittered embellishments is not only a fun and relatively simple technique, it also is budget-friendly. It allows you to create just the size and color of embellishment needed no matter what project you are working on.

You Will Need:

- Stampin' Up! strawberry slush cardstock
- Sparkle N Sprinkle starfire glitter
- Marvy Clever Lever flower punch
- Scrapbook Adhesives by 3L® adhesive sheets

1. Peel the backing from the adhesive sheet. Press the sheet onto a piece of cardstock just bigger than the punch or die you plan to use. Press the entire area firmly to be sure the adhesive is fully adhered to the cardstock (Photo 1).

2. Slowly begin to peel away the paper backing left on the opposite side of the adhesive. Take care to pull evenly so as to allow even removal of the backing without removing the adhesive (Photo 2).

3. Cover the entire piece with glitter and press gently to be sure it sticks to the uncovered adhesive (Photo 3).

4. Remove the excess and check to be sure the entire sheet has been covered well in glitter (Photo 4).

5. Punch the desired shape from the now glitter-covered cardstock (Photo 5).

The final piece can be adhered as is to any project or can be further altered and shaped as in the final project shown (Photo 6).

Note: *While this step-by-step shows how to do this technique using a simple flower punch, any punch or die can be used to create glittered embellishments.*

Never Forgotten

1. Form a 5 x 7-inch card from navy cardstock.

2. Cut a 4½ x 6½-inch piece from light orange cardstock. Using photo as a guide, punch approximately 12 circles from double-sided adhesive sheet. Peel off one side of protective backing from each circle and attach to top half of panel. Remove remaining backings; sprinkle circles with glitter and tap off excess.

3. Cut a 4½ x 1-inch piece from white patterned paper; adhere to panel. Wrap ribbon around panel as shown; tie in a bow. Adhere panel to pink cardstock; trim a small border. Adhere to card front.

4. Stamp sentiment on card front. Trace the word "Glitter" with adhesive pen; sprinkle with glitter and tap off excess.

5. Cut four 1-inch squares from blue patterned paper. Adhere each square to pink cardstock; trim a small border. Adhere squares to white cardstock in a square pattern as shown; trim a small border. Adhere to card front.

6. Apply adhesive from an adhesive sheet to a 2½ x 2½-inch piece of pink cardstock; sprinkle glitter onto adhesive and tap to remove excess.

7. Punch a flower from glitter-coated panel; trim between petals and shape so petals overlap slightly. Attach button to flower center using adhesive dot. Attach flower to card front using foam square.

Designer's Tip:
Adding just a hint of interest to the sentiment is as simple as using the glue pen to highlight a single word and shaking just a dusting of glitter over top.

Materials
- Stampin' Up! cardstock: night of navy, strawberry slush, crisp cantaloupe, whisper white
- Die Cuts With A View Coral and Navy 12 x 12 paper pad
- Jillibean Soup Butterflies stamp set
- Stampin' Up! strawberry slush ink pad
- Sparkle N Sprinkle starfire glitter
- 18 inches ½-inch-wide white seam binding
- Dark blue button
- Punches: Marvy Clever Lever (2-inch flower); ½-inch circle
- Scor-Pal double-sided adhesive sheets
- Scrapbook Adhesives by 3L® adhesive sheets
- Adhesive pen
- Paper adhesive

Those who leave a trail of *Glitter* are never forgotten

Adhesive Glitter Background

Punching through a sheet of double-sided adhesive, applying the punched shapes to a cardstock panel, and then covering them with glitter is a great way to create your own glitter-embellished cardstock. An even simpler approach is making stripes by applying tape runner and covering that in glitter. Don't limit it to just a clear translucent glitter; think of all the fun you could have making each dot a different color or every other stripe a different color!

You Will Need:
- Stampin' Up! crisp cantaloupe cardstock
- Sparkle N Sprinkle starfire glitter
- Marvy ½-inch circle punch
- Scor-Pal double-sided adhesive sheets

1. Begin by punching circles from the double-sided adhesive sheet. Peel one side and press the circles firmly onto the cardstock (Photo 1).

2. Trim any excess that hangs over the edge and peel away the backing to expose the adhesive layer (Photo 2).

3. Cover the entire panel with glitter and press the glitter onto the exposed adhesive (Photo 3).

4. Remove the excess glitter to reveal the glittered background (Photo 4). ✘

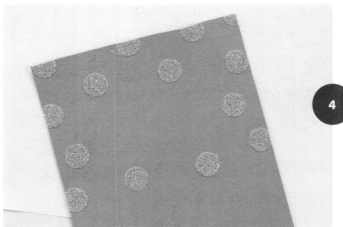

Heat Embossing

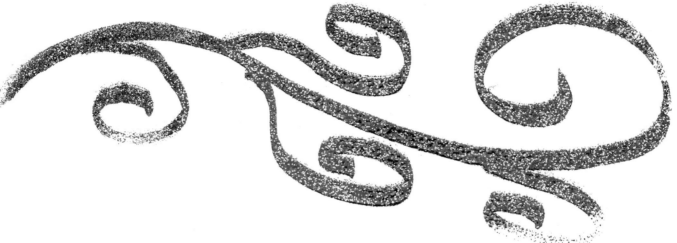

"The purpose of art is washing the dust of daily life off our souls."

—Pablo Picasso

A wonderful technique that lends both interest and texture to any project is heat embossing. Heat embossing can be used to create beautiful main images, awesome backgrounds and fabulous texture, and it is the jumping-off point for many additional artistic techniques. You may have seen various "thicknesses" of embossing powder. Generally, you will see regular embossing powder which is for "general" or "all-purpose" application.

A "fine" or "detail" embossing powder would be used for fine line art or highly detailed images. And there is also the opposite extreme found in "thick" or "ultra-thick" embossing powders, often used in sturdy pieces such as wearable paper-art pieces and home decor. In this book I have decided to teach the basics, a twist on the basics and just a few additional stepped-up techniques to highlight the versatility of heat embossing.

Embossing Basics

You Will Need:
- Stampin' Up! very vanilla cardstock
- Stampin' Up! Backyard Basics stamp set
- Ink pads: Stampin' Up! (coastal cabana); Imagine Crafts/Tsukineko VersaMark (watermark)
- Clearsnap Top Boss black embossing powder
- Embossing heat tool
- Water brush

1. Begin by using VersaMark watermark ink or embossing ink to stamp multiple images (Photo 1).

2. Cover with black embossing powder (Photo 2).

3. Gently turn the paper over to remove the excess and place it back in the open container; seal it before moving on to the next step (Photo 3).

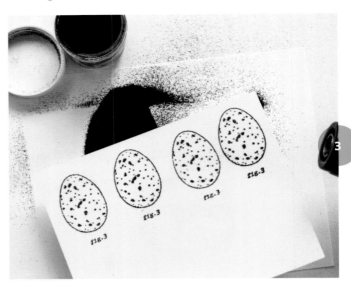

4. Turn the tool on and hold it for a few moments to allow it to fully heat up. For finer detailed images such as this one, I like to heat from the back side of the cardstock so as to not blow the embossing powder off the image and have it melt elsewhere on the project accidentally. Heat until you see the granules of embossing powder melt and become shiny. Once cooled, you will feel that the surface is smooth and glossy (Photo 4).

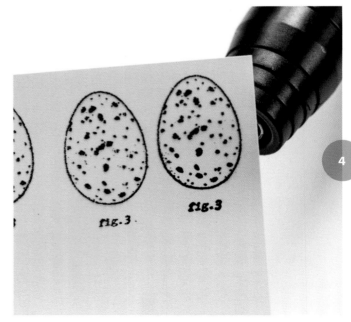

Embossing Basics With a Twist

While the steps are relatively similar, stamping the image with a slow-drying ink such as a pigment ink—instead of a VersaMark watermark ink or embossing ink—allows you to emboss the ink in clear embossing powder. You can purchase only one embossing powder but have a host of colors to choose from, depending on what colors of slow-drying pigment inks you already own!

1. Using black pigment ink, stamp the image multiple times (Photo 5).

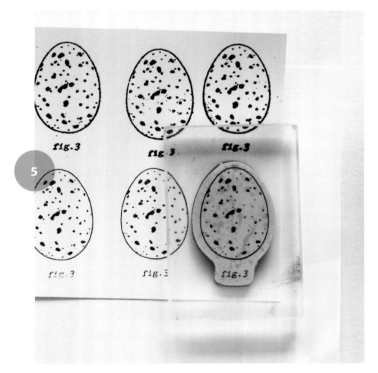

2. Use clear embossing powder to fully cover the images (Photo 6).

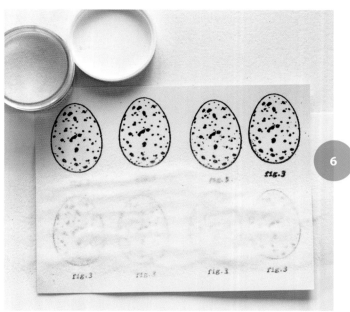

3. Gently turn the paper over to remove the excess and place it back in the open container; seal it before moving on to the next step (Photo 7).

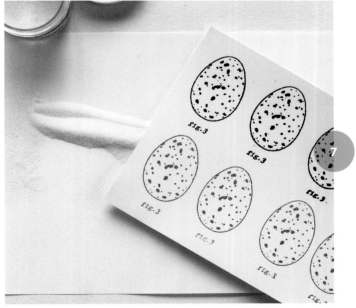

4. This time, heat from above and watch as the embossing powder heats and melts, turning from granular to smooth (Photo 8).

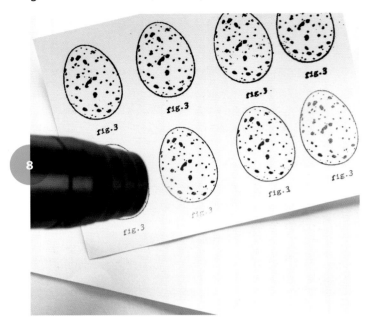

5. Take the sheet of embossed images and use a wide flat brush and water to "wash" diluted ink onto the images quickly and efficiently (Photo 9).

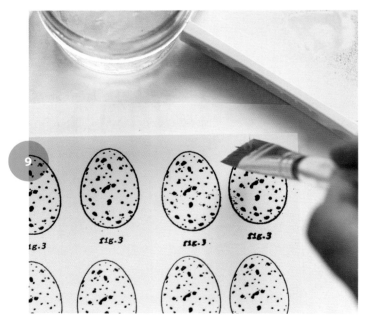

6. Repeat the color application until the desired depth of color is reached. You now have multiple images that can be cut out and used on future projects (Photo 10).

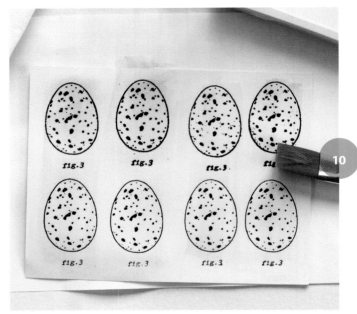

Note: *Another little tip to help you really think outside the box and lend versatility to your technique repertoire: As an alternative to using white pigment ink for the background image, try stamping with bleach or perhaps using VersaMark watermark ink to create a tone-on-tone look (Photo 11).*

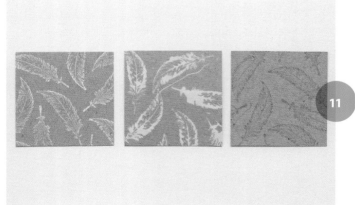

Materials

- Cardstock: Stampin'
  Up! (coastal cabana,
  chocolate chip,
  very vanilla); Bazzill
  Basics (kraft)
- Stampin' Up! stamp
  sets: Fine Feathers,
  Backyard Basics,
  Banner Banter
- Scrap paper
- Ink pads: Stampin'
  Up! (coastal
  cabana); Clearsnap
  pigment (frost
  white); Imagine
  Crafts/Tsukineko
  VersaMark
  (watermark),
  Memento (rich
  cocoa)
- Clearsnap Top Boss
  black embossing
  powder
- 18 inches ⅝-inch-
  wide cream
  grosgrain ribbon
- Want2Scrap amber
  self-adhesive
  rhinestones
- Embossing heat tool
- Water brush
- Sewing machine
  with cream thread
- Scrapbook
  Adhesives by 3L®
  adhesive foam
  squares
- Double-sided tape
- Paper adhesive

You're the Best

1. Form a 4¼ x 5½-inch card from aqua cardstock.

2. Cut a 3⅞ x 5⅛-inch piece from kraft cardstock. Using photo as a guide, stamp top section with feather images using white ink.

3. Cut a 3⅞ x ⅞-inch piece from aqua cardstock; apply double-sided tape horizontally across center. Rumple-fold ribbon, pressing into adhesive; machine-stitch in place. Adhere ribbon strip to kraft panel, adhering ends of ribbon to back of panel. Adhere panel to brown cardstock; trim a small border. Adhere to card front.

4. Ink banner image using brown ink; stamp twice onto scrap paper without reinking; stamp a third time onto cream cardstock. Stamp sentiment onto banner using brown ink; cut out. Adhere to card front.

5. Stamp egg image onto cream cardstock using watermark ink. Sprinkle with embossing powder; heat-emboss. Color image using water brush and blue ink. Cut out; attach to card front using foam squares.

6. Attach gems to card front. ✗

Emboss Resist

You Will Need:

- Stampin' Up! whisper white cardstock
- Hampton Art Stamp and Stencil Butterflies stamp set
- Ink pads: Stampin' Up! (strawberry slush, crisp cantaloupe); Imagine Crafts/Tsukineko VersaMark (watermark)
- Clearsnap Top Boss clear embossing powder
- Craft sponge
- Embossing heat tool
- Paper towels

1. Use VersaMark watermark ink or embossing ink to stamp images randomly onto the surface of the panel. Cover with embossing powder, remove excess and heat to emboss (Photo 1).

2. Use a sponge to swipe and pounce orange ink lightly over the images. Leave some white areas for the second color application (Photo 2).

3. Once again use a sponge to pounce color over the stamped images. Here I have pounced the sponge first onto my scrap paper so as to not apply the ink too quickly or too deeply (Photo 3).

4. Use a slightly moistened paper towel to wipe the excess ink off of the surface of the embossed images (Photo 4).

5. Be sure to remove the ink from each image to better show off the finished emboss resist design (Photo 5).

You Make My Heart Flutter

1. Form a 4 x 9½-inch card from kraft cardstock.

2. Cut a 3¾ x 9¼-inch piece from white cardstock. Using photo as a guide, stamp bottom 5½-inch portion of panel using desired stamps and watermark ink. Sprinkle with embossing powder; heat-emboss.

3. Sponge panel with pink and orange inks. Using a slightly moist paper towel, remove excess ink from surface of embossed images.

4. Cut a 3¾ x 3¼-inch piece from yellow-and-white striped paper; adhere to top of embossed panel.

5. Cut a 3¾ x 1-inch piece from striped paper; adhere to embossed panel as shown.

6. Wrap panel with ribbon; tie in a bow. Adhere panel to card front.

7. Die-cut a 3¼ x 3⅛-inch Labels Nine shape from navy cardstock; adhere to card front.

8. Die-cut a 2⅝ x 2½-inch Labels Nine shape from white cardstock; stamp sentiment using charcoal ink. Using pink and orange inks and water brush, color the word "HEART"; let dry. Use adhesive pen to apply adhesive to the word "HEART"; sprinkle with glitter and tap off excess. Let dry. Attach to card front using foam squares.

9. Thread buttons with hemp cord; tie in a knot. Attach to card front using adhesive dots. ✘

Materials

- Cardstock: Bazzill Basics (kraft); Stampin' Up! (whisper white, night of navy)
- Hampton Art KI Memories Playlist 6 x 6 paper pad
- Stamp sets: Jillibean Soup (Butterflies); Hampton Art (Stamp and Stencil Butterflies)
- Ink pads: Stampin' Up! (strawberry slush, crisp cantaloupe); Clearsnap Chalk (charcoal); Imagine Crafts/Tsukineko VersaMark (watermark)
- Clearsnap Top Boss clear embossing powder
- Sparkle N Sprinkle starfire glitter
- 18 inches ⅝-inch-wide white seam binding
- 2¾-inch yellow buttons
- Hemp cord
- Spellbinders™ Labels Nine die templates (#S4-233)
- Die-cutting machine
- Craft sponge
- Paper towels
- Embossing heat tool
- Water brush
- Scrapbook Adhesives by 3L® adhesive foam squares
- Adhesive dots
- Adhesive pen
- Paper adhesive

Embossing Faux Metal

You Will Need:

- Stampin' Up! whisper white cardstock
- Stampin' Up! Amazing Birthday stamp set
- Imagine Crafts/Tsukineko VersaMark watermark ink pad
- Clearsnap Top Boss silver embossing powder
- Embossing heat tool

1. Begin with a panel of cardstock larger than you will need. Turn the VersaMark watermark ink pad over and press it gently along the top edge of the panel, leaving the bottom free to use as a "handle" of sorts in later steps (Photo 1).

2. Cover the ink with silver embossing powder, remove the excess and place it back in open container; seal it before moving on to the next step (Photo 2).

3. Heat the embossing powder just until it melts. Allow it to cool (Photo 3).

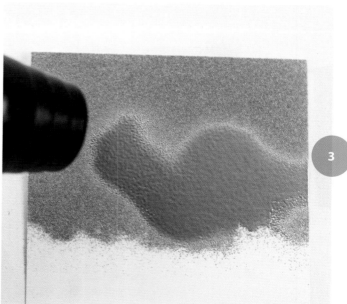

4. Once cool, apply a second coat of VersaMark watermark ink and a second layer of embossing powder. Heat just until melted (Photo 4).

5. Repeat step 4 but this time prior to heating, open the VersaMark watermark ink and press the stamp onto the ink pad. Allow it to sit nearby as you heat and melt the embossing powder for the third and final time (Photo 5).

6. Once the entire surface is melted, quickly press the stamp into the surface of the embossing powder. Allow it to sit for a moment (Photo 6).

7. Lift the stamp away to reveal your faux metal image. The VersaMark watermark ink acts as a releasing agent, allowing the stamp to lift easily from the cooled embossing powder and leaving a perfect impression in its place (Photo 7).

Note: If you find after all that work you don't get a good clear impression, don't despair! Simply reheat the entire panel and allow it to cool. Apply another layer of ink and embossing powder and repeat the last step to try for a better impression.

Happy Birthday to You!

1. Form a 5 x 7-inch card from gray cardstock.

2. Cut a 4½ x 6½-inch piece from circle patterned paper. Cut a 4½ x 2-inch piece from green patterned paper; adhere to panel as shown. Adhere to black cardstock; trim a small border.

3. Cut a 5 x 1-inch piece from navy cardstock; crimp with paper crimper. Adhere to panel folding and adhering ends to back. Wrap panel with baker's twine; tie in a knot. Thread button with baker's twine; attach to center of knot using adhesive dot. Adhere panel to card front.

4. Ink banner image with gray ink; stamp onto scrap paper. Stamp image onto white cardstock without reinking; cut out. Using photo as a guide, ink sentiment with markers and black ink pad; stamp onto banner. Attach banner to card front using foam squares.

5. Cut a 2 x 2-inch piece from white cardstock; apply watermark ink to piece by pressing pad onto cardstock. Sprinkle inked area with embossing powder; heat-emboss. Repeat inking and embossing two more times to create three layers of embossing powder. Apply watermark ink to cake stamp. Heat the embossed cardstock with heat tool; press inked stamp onto heated surface. Remove stamp and allow piece to cool. Punch out image using circle punch. Attach to card front using foam squares. ✗

Designer's Tip:
If a paper crimper is unavailable, texture can be added using an embossing folder or scoring tool. The blue cardstock strip can also be left smooth.

Materials
- Cardstock: Bazzill Basics (gray); Stampin' Up! (whisper white, night of navy, basic black)
- Die Cuts With A View Limoncello 12 x 12 paper pad
- Scrap paper
- Stampin' Up! Amazing Birthday stamp set
- Imagine Crafts/ Tsukineko ink pads: Memento (tuxedo black, London fog), VersaMark (watermark)
- Clearsnap Top Boss silver embossing powder
- Tombow markers: warm grey, hunter green, midnight blue
- The Twinery stone baker's twine
- ½-inch green button
- Embossing heat tool
- Paper crimper
- EK Success 1⅜-inch circle punch
- Scrapbook Adhesives by 3L® adhesive foam squares
- Adhesive dots
- Paper adhesive

HAPPY
HAPPY
HAPPY
HAPPY
BIRTHDAY
TO YOU!

Paper-Crafting Basics

Paper

Cardstock is thicker and heavier than regular paper and provides a sturdy surface or base for greeting cards and tags. Most card makers prefer to use at least an 80–100 lb. cardstock for their card bases and lighter-weight varieties for layering.

Cardstock is also available in smooth and textured assortments.

Both options can be used for bases and layering; however, if your design includes stamped images or sentiments, you will want to use a smooth cardstock to get the best image possible.

Scoring

A basic scored line is either a depressed or raised line that is created where you want to fold your card. Whether you use a stylus, bone folder or specially created scoring board and tool to create scored lines, the process is virtually the same. Use even pressure and draw the tool down the paper. If you are using a heavy-weight cardstock, you may want to go over the scored line twice.

Scored lines can also be used to create both mountain and valley folds as well as decorative lines to enhance your paper-craft designs.

Die-Cutting

Manual die-cutting machines and die templates make it easy to create special cut shapes directly in your card bases or to use as embellishments. These handy tools eliminate the need for detailed hand cutting and make fast work of creating die-cut pieces. Following the manufacturer's instructions, simply assemble the cutting plates and material that will be cut and run the layered plates through the machine to produce perfectly cut shapes.

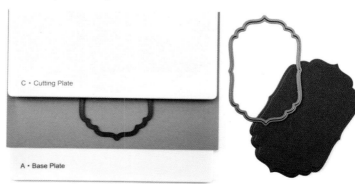

Also available are electronic die-cutting machines like the Cricut® that cut a wide variety of materials, including paper, vinyl, fabric and more. These machines make it easy to create cut shapes using the fonts on your own computer or the designs available from the manufacturer. Improved technology even allows you to create custom-cut shapes.

Adhesives

An extensive variety of adhesive products are available to use for your card and tag projects. Each glue or adhesive is formulated for a particular use and specified surfaces. With all adhesives, read the label and follow the manufacturer's directions for best results.

Dry adhesives are generally the preferred choice with paper crafters; they are easy to apply and require no drying time. The most common types of dry adhesives are double-sided adhesive tabs, tape and tape runners. These products are available in an assortment of sizes and styles. They are often packaged in easy-to-use dispensers, and they can be used on a wide variety of surfaces, including fabric.

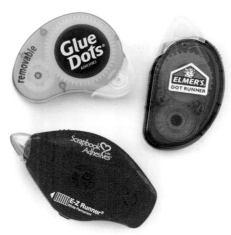

Dimensional adhesives, available as foam tabs and tape and adhesive dots, are another form of dry adhesive that are used to layer elements and create dimension. These products provide a strong hold and can be used with paper and fabric as well as hard embellishments.

Wet adhesives typically offer a strong hold and are often the most economical choice. Wet adhesives are formulated to work best with paper, foam, felt and hard embellishments such as beads and wooden buttons. When applying a wet adhesive to paper, keep in mind that too much wet adhesive may cause your paper to wrinkle or curl. ✖

Buyer's Guide

Bazzill Basics Paper Inc.
(800) 879-5185
www.bazzillbasics.com

Buttons Galore & More
(856) 753-6700
www.buttonsgaloreandmore.com

Clearsnap Inc.
(800) 448-4862
www.clearsnap.com

Copic®/Imagination International Inc.
(541) 684-0013
www.copicmarker.com

Die Cuts With A View
(801) 224-6766
www.diecutswithaview.com

EK Success
(888) 294-3929
www.eksuccessbrands.com

Faber-Castell USA Inc.
(800) 311-8684
www.fabercastell.com

Fantasia
www.fantasiapencil.com

Gamblin Artist Colors
(503) 235-1945
www.gamblincolors.com

Hampton Art
(800) 981-5172
www.hamptonart.com

Imagine Crafts/Tsukineko
(425) 883-7733
www.tsukineko.com

Impression Obsession Inc.
(877) 259-0905
www.iostamps.com

Jillibean Soup
(888) 212-1177
www.jillibean-soup.com

Marvy Uchida of America Corp.
(800) 541-5877
www.uchida.com

Morex
(800) 466-7393
www.morexcorp.com

Pebbles Inc.
www.pebblesinc.com

Prismacolor
(800) 346-3278
www.prismacolor.com

Queen & Co.
(858) 613-7858
www.queenandcompany.com

Really Reasonable Ribbon
www.reasonableribbon.com

Reeves
www.reeves-art.com

Royal & Langnickel
(800) 247-2211
www.royalbrush.com

Scor-Pal Products
(877) 629-9908
www.scor-pal.com

Scrapbook Adhesives by 3L®
(847) 808-1140
www.scrapbook-adhesives.com

Sparkle N Sprinkle
(888) 901-9173
www.sparklensprinkle.com

Spellbinders™ Paper Arts
(888) 547-0400
www.spellbinderspaperarts.com

Stampin' Up!
(800) STAMP UP (782-6787)
www.stampinup.com

Tombow USA
(800) 835-3232
www.tombowusa.com

The Twinery
www.thetwinery.com

Want2Scrap
(260) 740-2976
www.want2scrap.com

The Buyer's Guide listings are provided as a service to our readers and should not be considered an endorsement from this publication.

Annie's *Coloring Techniques for Paper Crafts* is published by Annie's, 306 East Parr Road, Berne, IN 46711. Printed in USA. Copyright © 2014 Annie's. All rights reserved. This publication may not be reproduced in part or in whole without written permission from the publisher.

RETAIL STORES: If you would like to carry this publication or any other Annie's publication, visit AnniesWSL.com.

Every effort has been made to ensure that the instructions in this publication are complete and accurate. We cannot, however, take responsibility for human error, typographical mistakes or variations in individual work. Please visit AnniesCustomerCare.com to check for pattern updates.

ISBN: 978-1-57367-531-4
1 2 3 4 5 6 7 8 9

WITHDRAWN
WATERFORD CITY AND COUNTY LIBRARIES